The Critical Twenty

20 Critical Steps to Business Success

Aaron Scott Young

"The Critical Twenty"

20 Critical Steps to Business Success

by

Aaron Scott Young

 This publication was created in the United States of America!
Photography by Alannah Avelin - www.AlannahVision.com

Created by 'Create a Book Program'
Book Title by Aaron Scott Young
Library of Congress Cataloging-in-Publication Data
ISBN: 978-0-692-40708-0
The opinions expressed in this book are the opinions of the Author and are not necessarily the opinions of Create a Book Program.

Read what others are saying about *Aaron Scott Young...*

"When Teddy Roosevelt spoke about "the man who is actually in the arena" in 1910, he was speaking about people like Aaron Young. Aaron is a man you meet and instantly trust. He is neither capable of guile or duplicity. He is simply an honest and forthright man of business - the kind of man your father did business with, and your grandfather before him. He is what America was built upon; solid, honest, thoughtful and God- fearing. Any person who has an opportunity to do business with Aaron needs to know what a rare find he is. A man not without imperfections, but a man at peace willing to do what's best for his friends, his partners and his family in every single case without exception and without hesitation. It is a privilege to be asked to endorse Aaron and to stand ready to provide further proof of his intelligence, talents and integrity."

Nathaniel Clevenger,
CEO M2 & Co

"Aaron rocked *Fire Nation* & his message will rock you. If you get to work with Aaron, your business better be prepared to IGNITE!"

John Lee Dumas,
Entrepreneur on Fire

"I consider Aaron Young one of the finest business thinkers I know. He is relentless in his pursuit of meaningful value that he can create in products and partnerships. He possesses a clarity of thought and an ability to focus that I find rare and inspiring. He is also one of the most ethical people I know. He takes amazing pains to ensure that he operates with integrity and with the interests of his partners and customers in mind."

Bill Kelly,
CEO & Co-founder, ReelDx, WebMD, Learning.com

"Aaron and I have worked closely together on many different projects since 1993. We have experienced the highs and lows that come with owning and operating businesses. Through it all Aaron has been a source of integrity and reason. He has an innate ability to think through complex issues, reduce them down to key fundamentals and then formulate action plans that provide results. His ability to relate to, understand and motivate people has been invaluable in our sales and marketing efforts. I highly recommend Aaron Young!"

Lee Morgan,
Co-Owner & COO Laughlin Associates

"I don't walk, but I run to share the stage with Aaron Young! What I find is that not only does he bring amazing knowledge to the table, but he makes it fun and really interactive to learn from him!"

Speaker Erik "Mr. Awesome" Swanson,
Secret Habitudes

"I have had the opportunity to work alongside Aaron for several years and to see the passion and the commitment he shows for the service he provides to his customers and clients. He is a gifted businessman, has high integrity, is an awesome family man, and brings value to the projects and services he offers his customers and clients. Aaron is the real deal and I am fortunate to have him as a friend and as a business resource."

John Chambers, CPA
Isler Northwest LLC CPA's and Business Advisors

"It's difficult to read the label from the inside of the bottle. As a small business owner, I often can't see beyond my nose. Aaron Young has been instrumental in enlightening a pathway to truths in my business. Every business owner should have a coach like Aaron!"

Michael Drew,
Author and CEO at Promote-A-Book

Aaron Young is a senior faculty member at our CEO Space International Conferences. His new book is a "must read". The CRITICAL TWENTY is a 7 Habits, The Secret, and Who Moved My Cheese kind of book. Anyone owning a business or thinking of entering into business ownership simply MUST read it. All of our CEO SPACE clan must read this book along with Chicken Soup and Rich Dad Poor Dad readers - do NOT miss this book or any book Aaron puts out - its packed with solid how-to-really-do-it wisdom for the C Suite!

Berny Dohrmann,
Author, Film producer, Founder CEO SPACE, Forbes #1 Conference for Small Business Owners

Preface

I have been an entrepreneur for 37 years. For 20 of those years I've been specifically focused on working with business owners.

As I celebrated my 50th birthday I wondered what I could do to help shorten the learning curve for other entrepreneurs. This little book is one of the answers that I arrived at. It's a short, easy read. But don't be fooled by the brevity. If you will really pay attention to what I've given you and then go and act on what you've learned, your business and your life will change. The concepts here are based on actual experience in the trenches.

I hope that these lessons will make your business adventures a little less scary and a lot more profitable.

Table of Contents

Step #1: Invent or Improve

Many people have technical skills or talent in a particular industry, but that is usually not enough to be truly successful as an entrepreneur. The critical first step to business success is to have a clever idea with a unique perspective. Success comes from making the consumer's life better—either by creating a product or service that isn't currently available, or improving upon an existing one.

For instance, an engineer can design and develop a vacuum cleaner because the mechanics of it are simple and straightforward. But can that vacuum revolutionize an industry? Consider the introduction of the Dyson vacuum. Why would anyone think consumers would pay two, three, or even four times as much for an odd-looking product that theoretically does the same thing as their current vacuum? It's easy to believe their success is based on a new, unique technology, but the reality is it's because of the benefits to the end user. It never loses suction and its swivel ball design makes a chore into a breeze—two key features with exceptional benefits.

How to Invent or Improve:

Ask yourself how you can apply your expertise to creating or improving a product or service that will benefit the consumer.

What would make the consumer's life better: more convenient, provide a better result, a savings of cost and time…less stress in their daily life?

What are some common complaints your current customers have about products or services?

How can your service help make your customer's business more money?

What frustrations do you or your family members have about a product or service? You can be the answer to your own problem, as well as for millions of other people!

Step #2: Determine and Define Your Market

Once you have your clever idea, determine if there is a market for your product or service. So many fortunes have been lost and dreams dashed when people rush into building the "next big thing", only to find out that no one is interested.

Consider this scenario: a first-time author excitedly explained to her literary agent how she spent the last two years writing this fabulous book about dating for men. She believed it would be a great success because there were no other books like it on the market.

The reality is, there's a reason her book would be the only one like it on the bookshelf—men don't buy books about how to date. There is no market for her material and thus no need for her product. Luckily, her savvy agent advised her on how to edit her book, change the name and market it to women, which landed her a publisher and a space on the bookstore shelf.

How to Determine and Define Your Market:

Do your market research. In tangible ways, clarify if there is a market for your product.

Check out the existing competition—you don't have to reinvent the wheel, just make it better!

- What do they offer?
- Who is their target audience?
- How do they market to that demographic?

Now think in terms of how you can distinguish yourself and gain market share.

Step #3: Devise Your Plan

Now that you've determined there is a need for your offering, it's time to make a plan of action. If we just wing it, we will almost certainly fail. However, if we have a specific goal in mind and work backwards to design a plan, we have a much greater likelihood of hitting our mark. How are you going to take your product or service to the market? How will you position your message in such a way that the market can respond? How will you keep track of the data you are gathering?

Determine who might be ideal partners or resources for you. Will they be joint ventures or affiliates?

Will you be using direct marketing, social media, etc.?

Examine all of the different ways you can not only engage the market but also what types of resources you will need— money, licensing, etc.—and include that in your plan.

How to Devise Your Plan:

Consider some of these ways to get moving:

Create a mind map of all of the possible spokes of the wheel, with the goal in the center. Continue to add sub-spokes to each section as ideas come to you.

Develop a list of benchmarks for the overall goal so that no section feels overwhelming and prevents you from moving forward.

Write out action items for each day and week and be realistic with your time so you don't burn out.

As you'll see from the next critical step, you don't need to know the how, just the what.

"When we deal in generalities, we shall rarely have success. When we deal in specifics, we shall rarely have failure."

- Thomas S. Monson

Step #4: Articulate Your Vision

Whenever I speak around the country, the very first thing I teach business owners is you need to be able to write a clear vision (one or two pages) that specifically articulates what your business would look like if it was functioning perfectly—right now, today.

When you can clearly state your vision and explain what you are working towards, you'll be amazed at how opportunities open up. People will cross your path, introductions will be made, books will be handed to you, a TED talk or podcast will be recommended to you. All of these serendipitous events will help you make quantum leaps toward achieving that vision.

In my experience, when I know exactly what I'm working toward, the path lines up before me and I'm able to make a direct route to achieving my goal.

How to Articulate Your Vision:

Your vision statement should be written down—ideally in longhand because that engages a different part of the brain and makes a more visceral and emotional connection to your subconscious mind.

Write out your vision based on the answers to these questions:

- What does your workspace look like?
- Are there other people in the office with you?
- What is the attitude and atmosphere in the office?

- What does your day look and feel like?
- What type of customers, vendors, and partners are you working with?
- Are you doing business on a local, national, or international level?
- What amount of money are you making?
- What does your lifestyle look like?

Step #5: Inspire Others

As brilliant as you might be, as pristine as your vision might be, and as charismatic as you are in front of a crowd, the fact is you can't reach any lofty goal on your own. Working in a vacuum is almost never successful. Every successful individual you have ever heard of has an amazing team that is supporting and lifting him or her along the way.

When you craft a clear vision statement and learn how to communicate it, you'll begin to find people who resonate with your vision. It's critically important that you always keep that vision alive.

People need to feel excited and inspired by your vision and no matter how good they are, most people on your team will not know your vision as passionately as you do. Their job, regardless of how high they are in the company, will only be to fulfill a portion of your grand vision. That's why it's critical that you stay in front of your people in a motivating and inspiring way.

How to Inspire Others:

Every time you come into a meeting, get on a phone call, or communicate on a digital level, you have to continually and consistently remind people what your vision is, where they fit, and how they're doing.

Inspire them to give a little bit more of their heart and their imagination to the vision so they can help grow it with you.

Stay engaged with them. Consistently share what you are working on and why it matters. Collaborate on how they can participate and you'll be amazed at how many people will want to be a part of it.

Step #6: Know the Nuts and Bolts

I've met many people who are charismatic, inspirational individuals who do a terrific job of firing up a crowd or giving a motivational speech. And they can do OK in business.

But the highly successful business people who can steadily build a company over time and generate real wealth are the ones who surround themselves with great coaches and complementary team members. And these same great leaders always keep their hands on the pulse of the operations of the business. They don't simply rely on other people to know how the business should work. Powerful leaders understand there is a mechanical, formulated template of operations to build a thriving business and they stay connected on all levels.

How to Know the Nuts and Bolts:

Once you know exactly how your business operation works day in and day out, then you can begin to look at ways to tweak it by integrating in affiliates and by adding strategic alliances. You can't risk making those adjustments until you know what makes it all work in harmony. It is critically important that you understand the nuts and bolts of why your business works…in all areas.

- How does each piece fit together?
- How does the technology work?
- What makes a successful marketing campaign?

- What is the sales message and process?
- How do you coordinate every department and make sure everyone is on the same page?
- Have you developed reporting systems to easily inspect your expectations?

"No matter how far you've gone down a wrong road, turn back."

– Turkish Proverb

Step #7: Hire for More Than the Gap

Hire slowly, fire quickly. We've all heard it and it may sound a little harsh, but the people working for and with you will have a dramatic effect on the success or failure of your business. I've seen a variety of high-level mistakes made in the name of filling a gap. You know you do a poor job at something so you need to fill the gap.

Just because you find someone who appears bright, optimistic, and has the right educational pedigree doesn't mean he/she is the answer to your need. Also, simply hiring someone who is exceptional at what we believe we are not good at will not guarantee success.

What happens when you *do* hire the wrong person? If you've been in business for any length of time, you've seen it— employees who are not in sync with your vision. And, every time you see them, you can feel it in your gut. When this happens, you need to let them go, and quickly. Set them and yourself free to become more successful. You'll be doing both of you a favor.

How to Hire Wisely:

Be wise in the people you surround yourself with—make sure they understand and are supportive of your vision and are not holding you back from reaching your goal. Your job is to clearly define the goal assigned to your potential new hires, develop clear job parameters, and set them up to win.

- What is their task?
- What are the constraints in which they need to work?
- What technology will be available?
- What levels of authority and autonomy will be permitted in order to make certain decisions?
- What types of training and access to you will be available?
- How will they know if they are winning or losing?

Only then, will you be able to effectively interview and decide on the best person for the job.

Step #8: Train the Why

Once you've hired the right team, it is your obligation to train them and set them up to succeed.

I regularly coach business owners who have made a critical mistake. They are busy and since they really don't understand certain elements of the job, such as accounting or information technology, they end up hiring people and abandoning them to figure out their job duties on their own. This is a recipe for disaster.

Hiring people and then deserting them will make them feel tricked, lonely, and frustrated. If you leave your people alone to create within a vacuum, they will try their hardest to do what they think you want, but that doesn't ensure that they will help you reach your actual goals. Instead of contributing team members, you'll end up with unproductive, frustrated workers and so much turnover that you'll never have consistency and efficiency.

How to Train the Why:

Training is a collaborative process. You must train your people.

You don't need to know how they do their job, but you do need to communicate the Why.

Understand enough of what they do to have an intelligent conversation while you demonstrate how their position is incorporated into your vision.

Simply having them "shadow" another employee is not the answer. The result of this technique is a second-generation translation of your vision. It's your company, your vision, your goals—it's your responsibility to communicate the Why!

Schedule (and keep!) regular follow-up training meetings with all new hires so you can stay current on their progress and how they are integrating into your culture.

Step #9: Get Clear on Your Message

Why does this business matter?

A lot of small business owners I meet are so busy doing the work and trying to get the next deal that they lose track of why they started in the first place—their vision, mission, and goals.

They are too busy just chasing a sale instead of clearly communicating a message. Everyone in your market is only concerned with what's in it for them. Your customers' goal is not to make you successful—their intention is to reach ***their*** goals. They are looking to you to make something easier, to solve their problem, to make them happier, thinner, richer, etc.

Are you able to clearly articulate your message so they see you as the answer to realizing their goals? And are you able to do it in an ever-changing market?

How to Get Clear on Your Message:

Go back every year and ask the basic

questions again… Why do we

matter?

What's going on in the world?
What's going on in the public's mind?

How do we stay current?

Why will our product or service help our market be safer, healthier, wealthier, happier, etc.? How will engaging with us benefit them?

What worked for you two years ago will probably not work today. That's why McDonald's continuously changes their taglines for their hamburgers because they are constantly trying to find the right new message to keep us walking through their door instead of their competition's door.

"Advertising is like a magnet and is subject to the Law of Polarity. Specifically, your ad's ability to attract customers cannot exceed its potential to repel."

– Roy H. Williams

Step #10: Market with Concentrated Strategies

Most companies have a limited budget for marketing and after payroll it's often the largest line item on the P & L. When you are getting started, you are funding everything yourself through savings, loans, credit cards, etc., so it's important to use those funds wisely.

There are endless opportunities that will be presented to you to market your product or service but the broader you cast your net, the less successful your yield.

When you can get your marketing message dialed in so specifically that half the people who see your message run away from you, the other half will run toward you, latch on and never let go. And that's all you need to grow your business—just half.

How to Market with Concentrated Strategies:

- Who are my customers and where are they hanging out? Create two or three avatars that represent your customer. What do they look like?
- What websites do they visit?
- What Meet Up or networking opportunities do they take advantage of?
- Do they attend seminars?
- Are they mostly older people? If so, do they read print advertising?
- Do they spend time on obscure websites because of their hobbies, religious beliefs,

cultural mores, weight loss goals, conservative or liberal news outlets?

Use laser-focused marketing efforts—take your limited marketing dollars and figure out how to maximize them by putting them in the path of your ideal customer.

Step #11: Learn to Sell…and Keep Learning

No business can do anything until something gets sold. That's the simple truth.

You can be a master at everything else that's been mentioned here so far, but if you can't sell, you'll never have a customer.

From the top down, your business has to be able to sell. You don't have to be the best salesperson, but you have to understand the art and science of selling.

Although there are great books about selling, the truth is because your market and adapted message are ever-changing, you'll have to continue to create step-by-step mechanisms to sell your product or service.

How to Learn to Sell…and Keep Learning:

Marshal these three things:

1. The wisdom of the ages
2. The current successes
3. Your own daily experience

Make sure you learn the art of selling, keep studying the best practices from third parties who excel, and be an observer of your own methods of what you are saying. Where did your client jump in? When did their eyes light up, and when did they glaze over? Your weekly sales meetings (Yes, at least once a week!) should include discussions about what wins your team members had that week, and what language they used to turn the discussion in their favor in order to get the sale. Gather and share the best practices of each of your salespeople.

Write everything down and begin scripting out your process. A sales script does not have to be verbatim. It is simply an organized way of communicating that achieves your goals. Focus on and train your team members to follow the script and stick to best practices. Otherwise, you'll find yourself frustrated and poor.

Step #12: Be a True Advocate for Your Business

I was recently at an event in which awards were given out for the best sales producers of a well-known national insurance company. Interestingly, two top producers were a father and daughter who compete in the same market.

How did they have such phenomenal success? Their number one lead magnet for their businesses traveled everywhere they did. They and their team all drive company cars fully wrapped in professional-looking advertising that directs their potential clients to their office. Everywhere they went they brought with them a very bold branding message.

This is also true of a friend of mine who is one of the founders of WebMD. I don't ever remember seeing him without a WebMD logo on a shirt, hat, briefcase, etc. Everywhere he went he was a walking advertisement and advocate for his brand. The company he built is now a household name, he's made millions and he continues to wear his brand everywhere he goes.

How to be a True Advocate for Your Business

Are you an advocate?

Are you willing to open your mouth?

Are you willing to say, "I'm proud to be a part of this company and you might want to learn more about us"?

The people who are willing to be loud and proud about their brand are most likely the top-producing members of that company.

If you let your pride or ego get in the way, just be prepared to be a marginal producer rather than a superstar.

Never stop advocating for your business. Show your future customers you are proud of your company.

"You don't have to see the whole staircase, just take the first step."

–Martin Luther King, Jr.

Step #13: Exceed Your Promises

There are companies that make big promises, but when you actually attempt to engage them, they begin to disappoint. Your level of confidence in the big promise that was made in their marketing begins to dwindle.

It's always a pleasure to find a company that created a good promotion that brought you to the point of making the phone call, walking into their store, or going to their website. It's even better when, once you arrive, the good experience you expected turns into a great experience.

Remember that return clients and referrals will come when you under-promise and over-deliver, not the other way around. They expect you to do a good job. They expect you to deliver on your promise. And, if you give them just a little bit extra, they will become a disciple for your business. Word-of-mouth referrals are so much more valuable than general marketing leads. The business you receive will far exceed the nominal expense of any Nurture Campaign you develop. Here's a great example...

Exceeding Your Promises: Mercedes Benz Case Study

Years ago, I bought a brand new Mercedes Benz. I fully expected it to be a great-driving, well-equipped luxury experience, and there would be a certain level of prestige from owning it. I knew that if all of those promises were realized, my money would have been well spent. What I was not anticipating was having the brand go above and beyond my expectations in the form of a nurture campaign.

The day I picked up the car, there was a collection of branded gift items waiting for me inside the car. A few weeks later, I received two very nice Mercedes key chains in the mail. A few weeks after that, I received two logo-branded coffee mugs with gourmet coffee inside. The next package that arrived was a box of chocolates with the Mercedes Benz logo on it.

In the first two years of owning my car, I continued to receive little promotional gifts in the mail. In addition, every time I went into the dealership for service, I was offered espresso and chocolate-dipped cookies, and they detailed my car. They also offered massages and manicures while I waited for service. None of this was expected, and none of their Nurture Campaign is mentioned in their advertising—it is what they do above and beyond their already exceptional promises, and it turned me into a huge fan.

How to Exceed Your Promises:

Every experience I had with Mercedes Benz was a surprise and delight. It made me want to always own a Mercedes because any other car-buying experience would be a disappointment.

What are you doing with your customers to not just deliver what is expected, but to delight them once they make the decision to work with you? Are you finding simple ways to give them an experience that was unexpected and wonderful?

Are you making it difficult for them to consider ever doing business with your competition because they have become accustomed to how great you make them feel?

You can do something as simple as sending the customer a couple of gourmet brownies, engraving a picture frame with their name on it, or sending them a branded logo coffee mug. Give these extras without expecting anything in return. Don't just give them what they expected, but give them a little bit more—and remind them you are a great company.

Step #14: Create Strategic Alliances

There are companies that try to go it alone and others who go out and find alliances. Undoubtedly, there are already companies who are reaching your ideal client and are providing top-notch, complementary services to what you do. Figure out how you can cross-market to each other's client lists so that you both can be stronger together than you can ever be separate—that's the sign of a great strategic alliance.

Alliance partners can help you in critical ways:

1. Introduce you to your potential customer for a much lower cost than doing your own marketing

2. Reach a market you didn't already know
3. Teach you how to be successful in new markets
4. Provide you with third-party endorsement of your services

The fourth benefit listed above is reason enough to find an alliance partner. In essence, they will be trumpeting to the world that you are a worthy company to work with and they trust you enough to be associated with you and refer you to their clientele. This type of third-party endorsement is exponentially more powerful than anything you can say about your own company in your marketing efforts.

How to Create Strategic Alliances:

You'll see companies such as American Express use all types of strategic partners in their marketing efforts in the hopes that you will be motivated to sign up for their card and spend money with their partners to earn points and/or cash back.

Even small companies who are close in proximity can work together. You see it all of the time when retailers in the same shopping center provide discounts for each other's services and products.

Think of companies that have complementary products and services to yours.

Even the pizza place two doors down can help promote your frozen yogurt or cupcake shop.

Successful companies, on both the biggest and smallest levels, can lock arms and march forward faster with good strategic alliances.

Step #15: Keep Innovating

Your product, no matter how good it is, will eventually go stale. Your market will be interested in it for a while and then they will start looking for something or someone new who is offering a slightly different service.

For example, the movie industry has changed from reel-to-reel film, to VHS, to DVD, to streaming and on-demand. Technology and the delivery method will continue to change how customers consume service and products. It's important that you continue to innovate.

Innovation does not necessarily mean throwing out existing products and services, but determining what else can be done to stay fresh and interesting and growing in the marketplace.

Keep Innovating: Corning Case Study

Corning Cookware is a great example of continuous innovation. For many years, Corning dominated the market for top-quality glass pots and pans. But, over time, they started losing market share to similar products copied by foreign manufacturers that were being sold for much less than Corning could afford to compete with. Corning was on the verge of going out of business. They had less than six months before mass layoffs and plant closings began.

The board of directors got together to discuss the realization that they could not continue to be successful by simply repeating their current manufacturing process. They asked themselves, "How do we use all of our existing resources to do something totally different in order to survive?" They challenged their teams to come back with ideas on how to utilize their existing equipment on nights and weekends so as not to disturb their existing product line.

The result was 20 new ideas, one of which was to manufacture fiber-optic cable, which was a new concept at the time.

Corning Glass is now the number one manufacturer of fiber- optic cable in the world. Not only did this brainstorming technique save them from failure, but now it has become an annual strategic event.

In recent years, one of those mock survival meetings at Corning produced the idea of Gorilla Glass™. Corning's new venture is now the source of a large percentage of Smartphone screens worldwide.

How to Keep Innovating:

Who would have thought that a pots and pans manufacturer would be successful at fiber optics *and* Gorilla Glass™?

Anything is possible when it feels like we have very few options. In tough times, we stretch ourselves to survive. But what if you did the same type of brainstorming as Corning?

What technical, creative, or analytical skills that you currently use can be converted into new products and services?

How can you expand upon your present knowledge and/or gain new knowledge?

Who can you brainstorm with to think outside of your own business operations? You'll want to include your current team, but you might also want to engage with professionals outside of your industry for a fresh approach. A new set of eyes can be invaluable, especially during times of stress.

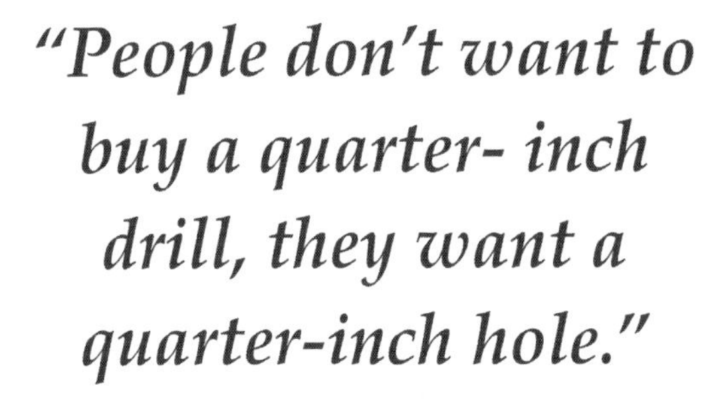

"People don't want to buy a quarter- inch drill, they want a quarter-inch hole."

- Theodore Levitt

Step #16: Empower Your Management Team to Fail Forward

Just as we talked about hiring the right people and spending time training them on the *why* of your mission, you also need to let them run.

Your management team should consist of people who play at the things you have to work at. Translation: they are smarter than you within certain areas of your operations. When you get these people on your team, you have an obligation to give them clear directions and then not hover over them.

If you micromanage everything your team does, your company will never be able to grow past you, your talents, and your understanding of technology and the markets. If you give your team the leeway to do things they think are right, you'll find your company is innovating in ways you never could have imagined on your own…even when they make mistakes.

How to Empower Your Management Team to Fail Forward:

One of the most critical elements of empowering your team is to give them the freedom to be an entrepreneur and put their own personal DNA on what they are doing—customer service, IT, sales, etc. Give them clear, bright lines that they can work within so they keep going in the direction of your vision, but within those lines; let them personalize what they are doing.

Management teams need to be empowered to magnify their stewardship and make use of their personalities. In addition, it's critical to give them the leeway to take chances and risk failure without reprisal. Not everything will work out as you hoped, but it's important that you don't have a tantrum and berate them because their decision has cost the business money. Allow them to figure out what works, what doesn't, and how to make smarter choices next time.

This will also be a positive teaching opportunity for the rest of the organization about taking some risks and making adjustments. The empowerment to fail forward is a tremendous confidence builder. Your team will love you if they know they can make choices and, when they don't work out, the failure can be used as a learning opportunity without punitive measures.

Step #17: Go on an Artist's Date

An Artist's Date is a concept that comes from a book entitled *The Artist's Way* by Julia Cameron.

You may have heard of this concept, but under a different name. No matter what you call it, it's critical that you—the leader, the visionary, the manager, the innovator—get out and away from the business on a regular basis.

Steve Jobs taught that most people with specific college training won't be great entrepreneurs because they tend to think in a very linear way. Entrepreneurship is all about connecting dots and, as Steve says, the more dots you have to connect the more likely you are to be really successful. When you take yourself on a date and get out of your business and go do something that is only for you, you'll release your imagination, refuel your enthusiasm, and discover more dots to connect—making everything in your life more successful.

How to Go on an Artist's Date:

At least once a week, go do something completely indulgent and fun.

For some people that means go wander through an art museum or attend an afternoon movie—without guilt.

I like to dig through thrift shops and garage sales or go horseback riding in the woods.

Do something that detaches your mind from everything related to the business. Give yourself a chance to engage different parts of your brain and think different thoughts.

Just relax and shake off the stresses that come from owning a business.

It doesn't matter if you're running a company with a thousand employees or you're a solo entrepreneur: you need to stay energized, alert, awake, and excited.

Step #18: Think of Your Company as an Asset

I speak to nearly 50,000 business owners each year through personal appearances, and many more through articles, interviews, blogs, and podcasts. I also have tens of thousands of clients of my own. Very often, when I meet business owners and I hear them talk about their company, they don't know where the company stops and they keep going, or vice versa.

Their life is completely entwined with their company. They think of it as their passion, their mission. Either way, it is utterly connected to their life, and is often referred to as their baby.

It's critically important to be passionate about your business and an advocate for it, but where you start making mistakes is when you stop thinking of your business as an asset that you own.

When you think of your company as an asset, you will begin to make intelligent decisions that will not only make you more money as the owner, but will also give you something to sell or pass down to the next generation so you can move on.

Begin with the end in mind. Always remember that you are not the corporation and the corporation is not you.

How to Think of Your Company as an Asset:

Look at it like you would a piece of real estate, or intellectual property—something you own that you are trying to leverage to its greatest potential and capacity so that it makes money, provides a great value to all stakeholders, and is worthy in the marketplace.

But, more importantly, when you start to think of your company as an asset, you'll start finding ways to organize it so it has value to other people. For instance, when you get bored with running this company or feel like things have gone stale, you'll want to have an asset that is salable—a business built on clear processes and mechanisms that will appeal to a buyer. It cannot be something that is solely tied to your abilities and your day-to-day work in the company.

Build a business that is bigger than you, one that other people would like to get their hands on, pay you for it, then take what you've done and expand it with their new vision.

"I was a singer in a younger age and one of my mentors taught me a valuable music and business lesson. First, you learn the sheet music and, once you completely master it, then you can improvise."

–Aaron Scott Young

Step #19: Keep Your Finances in Check

A lot of successful small companies run by the founder have a tendency to make several unwise financial decisions. The first, and most common, is keeping a long-time employee on payroll beyond their value. Payroll costs are often the highest expense of any company, and it's important that you try to keep your payroll costs down to 30 percent or less of your overall expenses. Marketing is another area to continuously assess. Test location and level of your marketing costs to ensure they are still producing significant leads.

In many closely-held companies, the owner pulls all of the profits out of the business. Although that is their right, a successful company will approach their finances in a different way. They get their cost of goods sold and product delivery expenses completely in check, and have a good idea of ROI on marketing and sales so they are driving great profits into the business. Lastly, it's important, as the CEO/owner of your small business, that you pay yourself a reasonable salary for the job you are doing. Clearly understand that if you were to replace yourself with a new person, what would you pay them to do your job? Then pay yourself that salary.

How to Keep Your Finances in Check:

Remember that you, as the owner, are different than you, as the employee. Once you've got your payroll, marketing, and COGS in check, and you're profitable, then it's time to look at what else you are doing with your finances.

How are you investing in new

products? How are you investing in

new technologies?

Are you making smart choices in risky ventures, and are you getting good ROI?

Keep money in your business—always have a slush fund or savings so you can weather storms and predetermine what portion of your cash reserves you are willing to use to take on new projects, develop new products, and invest in new marketing, etc. Learn to understand your financial reports and stick to your processes. Doing this will help you survive the bad months and celebrate the great ones!

Step #20: Know When to Replace Yourself

When a company first starts out, it's all about your idea, your vision, and your unique talents and how you can go out and really make a difference in the world. It's fun to be at those early stages to see your company take off, and it's a rush to know you can be a real player in your market.

If you are truly successful and getting to the goals you set, it's likely your company will eventually outgrow you. For a while, you'll be able to hire more experienced senior management to help innovate and stay on top of marketing trends and technology. But, the truth is, the personality that makes a great entrepreneur is rarely the same personality that makes an outstanding manager.

I've repeatedly seen a company grow to $5M, $20M or $50M in sales and the founder just stays on. What ends up happening is that the great management team that was built becomes frustrated. The entrepreneur doesn't know how to manage a company of such a large size, and he or she becomes a bottleneck to the company's continued success. The result is that a company will grow to a certain level, make money for a while, and then begin to sink, and eventually die, because the founder didn't know when to get out of the way.

Don't be afraid to give up the reins. Don't let ego or the need for accolades prevent you from trusting and empowering your people to be all they can be.

How to Know When to Replace Yourself:

Hire someone who is a better manager and has new, fresh ideas. You can stay on as the Chairman of the Board or some other leadership role.

Take the time, now, to look back to that original vision statement you made and realize, "We've made it happen. We're there now." Yes, you've made it happen, you've rung the bell, and now it's time to turn it over. Hand it over to a great manager, and take everything you've learned and move onto the next thing.

Recognize and honor this day. Celebrate it and step out of the way!

It's not over! As an entrepreneur, you always have new ideas and some new thing you want to chase, perhaps a new vision you want to bring to life.

Besides, what better way is there to celebrate your own success than by stepping down and starting something new?

In Closing…

One of the great joys of my life has been participating in lots of cool business ventures. Some worked. Many did not. As I head into my fourth decade as an entrepreneur, I am turning my attention to helping others learn from and, hopefully, avoid some of the mistakes I've made on my journey. This little book is like Cliff Notes for the real work that needs to be done. Dig deep and keep learning, and you will have a great experience, as I surely have.

If you want help with mastering any of the 20 Critical Steps outlined in this book and would like support in moving beyond your current level of success, please contact me. I welcome the opportunity to help your business thrive!

www.TheCriticalTwenty.com

I would like to dedicate this book to the best partner, in business and in life, a man could ever have…

my wife and true love, Michelle Young!

– Aaron Scott Young

Aaron Scott Young

For more than 20 years, Aaron Young has been empowering business owners to build strong companies and proactively protect their dreams. An entrepreneur with several multimillion-dollar companies under his own belt, Aaron has made it his life's work to arm other business owners with success strategies that immediately provide exponential growth and protection.

www.AaronScottYoung.com
www.laughlinusa.com

www.magnifyyourwealth.com

"The distilled wisdom and practical ideas in this book will save you hundreds of hours and thousands of dollars in achieving business success."

Brian Tracy,

Speaker & Best-Selling Author

Engage Aaron as Your Coach

Aaron has served as a strategic-thinking partner for hundreds of entrepreneurs and CEOs. As the CEO Laughlin Associates he's worked with more than 100,000 business owners across a wide range of industries.

Clients call on Aaron for his counsel and guidance in every aspect of business operations, including corporate structuring, asset management and protection, growth strategies, partnership issues, leadership, and corporate compliance. Aaron has witnessed first-hand both their common mistakes and common successes. He knows what works and what does not. He can help you avoid obstacles and help you find the fastest, safest path to success.

To learn more about working one-on-one with Aaron Young contact **aaronyoung@laughlinusa.com**

BONUS- Building Your Business on A Solid Foundation

You've proved you have the guts, passion and commitment to turn your dream into a reality. You are doing something millions of Americans only wish they could do: run their own business. But lets face the facts, it doesn't come without risk. As a small business owner you have unnecessary litigation, economic downturn, creditors and taxes to deal with, not to mention the millions of other things that could go wrong.

Putting together an asset protection plan is an essential part to any business and it doesn't have to be expensive or complicated. By structuring your business in a corporation or forming a limited liability company you can take advantage of a strong asset protection tool. Just the simple act of incorporating your business can protect your personal assets, reduce your taxes and provide numerous fringe benefits.

Complimentary SnapShot Review

Receive A Complimentary SnapShot Review of Your Business, a $399 Value, complimentary when you use the following link.

www.limitmyrisk.com

The SnapShot offers key indicators on how to grow, profit and protect your business.

www.limitmyrisk.com
1.800.648.0966

MAGNIFY YOUR WEATH- LIVE SUMMIT

Join Me LIVE

The Magnify Your Wealth Summit, is designed for business owners, entrepreneurs, real estate investors, gig works, and hobbyists who want to increase profits, protect their assets, and learn to grow their wealth by leveraging opportunities.

www.magnifyyourwealth.com
1.800.648.0966